Those 50 Lost Days and Nights

For my most dear and loving wife
Rosemarie for christmas

David Jaffin

Those 50 Lost Days and Nights

The books by Dr. David Jaffin are housed
by the special collections
of New York University's libraries

First published in the United Kingdom in 2024 by
Shearsman Books
PO Box 4239
Swindon
SN3 9FN

Shearsman Books Ltd Registered Office
30–31 St. James Place, Mangotsfield, Bristol BS16 9JB
(this address not for correspondence)

www.shearsman.com

ISBN 978-1-84861-879-4

Production, composition, & cover design: Edition Wortschatz,
a service of Neufeld Verlag, Neudorf bei Luhe/Germany
E-Mail info@edition-wortschatz.de, www.edition-wortschatz.de

Title photograph:
Hannelore Bäumler, Munich/Germany

Printed in Germany

Contents

With continuing thanks for
Marina Moisel
preparing
this manuscript

and to Hanni Bäumler
for her well-placed
photograph

If I had to classify my poetry, it could best be done through the classical known "saying the most by using the least". The aim is thereby set: transparency, clarity, word-purity. Every word must carry its weight in the line and the ultimate aim is a unity of sound, sense, image and idea. Poetry, more than any other art, should seek for a unity of the senses, as the French Symbolists, the first poetic modernists, realized through the interchangeability of the senses: "I could hear the colors of her dress." One doesn't hear colors, but nevertheless there is a sensual truth in such an expression.

Essential is "saying the most by using the least". Compression is of the essence. And here are some of my most personal means of doing so turning verbs into nouns and the reverse, even within a double-context "Why do the leaves her so ungenerously behind". Breaking words into two or even three parts to enable both compression and the continuing flow of meaning. Those words must be placed back together again, thereby revealing their inner structure-atomising.

One of my critics rightly said: "Jaffin's poetry is everywhere from one seemingly unrelated poem to the next." Why? Firstly because of my education and interests trained at New York University as a cultural and intellectual historian. My doctoral dissertation on historiography emphasizes the necessary historical continuity. Today we often judge the past with the mind and mood of the present, totally contrary to their own historical context. I don't deny the past-romanticism and classical but integrate them within a singular modern context of word-usage and sensibility. Musically that would place me within the "classical-romantic tradition" of Haydn, Mozart, Mendelssohn, Brahms and Nielsen but at the very modern end of that tradition.

My life historically is certainly exceptional. My father was a prominent New York Jewish lawyer. The law never interested me, but history always did. A career as a cultural-intellectual historian was mine-for-the-asking, but I rejected historical relativism. That led me to a marriage with a devout German lady – so I took to a calling of Jesus-the-Jew in post-Auschwitz Germany. For ca. two decades I wrote and lectured all over Germany on Jesus the Jew. Thereby my knowledge and understanding of both interlocked religions became an essential part of my being. History, faith and religion two sides of me but also art, classical music and literature were of essential meaning – so many poems on poetry, classical music and painting.

Then Rosemarie and I have been very happily married for 62 years now. Impossible that a German and Jew could be so happily married so shortly after the war? I've written love poems for her, hundreds and hundreds over those 62 years, not only the love poems, as most are, of the first and often unfulfilling passion, but "love and marriage go together like a horse and carriage". Perhaps too prosaic for many poets?

When did I become a poet? My sister Lois wrote reasonably good poetry as an adolescent. I, only interested in sports until my Bar Mitzvah, a tournament tennis and table-tennis player, coached baseball and basketball teams, also soccer.

My sister asked whether I'd ever read Dostoyevsky. I'd only read John R. Tunis sports books and the sports section of the *New York Times* so I answered "in which sports was he active?" She said, rather condescendingly, "If you haven't read Dostoyevsky, you haven't lived." So I went to the library for the very first time and asked for a book by this Dostoyevsky. I received *Poor People*, his first book, that made him world famous. My mother shocked to see me reading and most especially a book about poor people said, "David, don't read that it will make you sad, unhappy – we, living in Scarsdale, weren't after all, poor people. From there it went quickly to my Tolstoy, Hardy and so on. In music it started with the hit parade, then *Lost in the Stars*, then the popular classics and with 15 or 16 my Haydn, Mozart, Schütz, Victoria… And then at Ann Arbor and NYU to my artists, most especially Giovanni Bellini, Van der Weyden, Georges de la Tour, Corot and Gauguin…

But it was Wallace Stevens' reading in the early 50s in the YMHA that set me off – he didn't read very well, but his '13 Ways of Looking at a Blackbird', 'Idea of Order at Key West', 'Two Letters' (in *Poems Posthumous*), 'Peter Quince at the Clavier', 'The Snowman'… and the excellent obituary in *Time* magazine plus the letter he answered some of my poems with compliments but "you must be your own hardest critic". That pre-determined my extremely self-critical way with a poem. Please don't believe that prolific means sloppy, for I'm extremely meticulous with each and every poem.

My poems were published in the order written and I'm way ahead of any counting... The poem is a dia-logical process as everything in life. The words come to me not from me, and if they strike or possibly join-a-union then I become desperate, read long-winded poets like Paz to set me off – he's very good at odd times. Those poems need my critical mood-mind as much as I need their very specially chosen words – not the "magic words" of the romantics, but the cleansed words of Jaffin – Racine used only 500 words. My words too are a specially limited society, often used, but in newly-felt contexts.

O something very special: I have a terrible poetic memory. If I had a good one as presumably most poets, I'd write say one poem about a butterfly, and every time I see/saw a butterfly it would be that one, that poem. But I forget my poems, so each butter-fly, lizard, squirrel... is other-placed, other-mooded, other-worded, other-Jaffined. That's the main reason why I am most certainly the most prolific of all poets.

Shakespeare is the greatest of us: his sonnets live most from the fluency and density of his language. I advise all future poets to keep away from his influence and the poetic greatness of The Bible.

Yours truly
David Jaffin

P. S.: As a preacher the truth (Christ) should become straight-lined, timelessly so, but as a poet it's quite different. What interests me most are those contradictions which live deeply within all of us, not only in theory, but daily in the practice. And then the romantics have led me to those off-sided thoroughly poetic truths that mysteriously not knowing where that darkened path will lead us.

*"A foolish consistency is
the hobgoblin of little minds"*

(Emerson)

Christ offer

s us the only-
true-freedom Not

the-freedom-
for-ourselve

s but the-
freedom-from-

ourself.

Good modern

music reduces
sound from its

intrinsic-
elongat

ing-effect
s.

As Goya

Some special
artists as

Goya so many-
sided out of

time and place
that it remain

s difficult
to place them

just-right as
an-immovable-

statue.

"In the Mood"

When they
hit Glenn

Miller's plane
high over

Nazi-Germany
What kind of

mood was just-
then inhabit

ing his down-
fall.

Moral Seduct

ion Can one
call undress

ing a young
lady's past

moral-seduct
ion.

A Similar

Life–Death Per
spective For

S. L. the
well–

accountable
pupil first

at his funer
al meant (as

he later ex
plained) to

kill him
(when the law

allowed While
firmly stanced
to keep him

fast–alive
to the very–

end and/or
My last word

s before the
operation

"I'm prepared
now to die"

While the
surgeon respond

ed "We've
other–intent

ions–for–
you".

A fully

through-spok
en late Feb

ruary morning
left him

timely-intent
of its out-

spoken clarity
as if we had

n't become
less-than-

strangers
in the course
of its light-

encompassing-
expectat

ions.

Renamed

That patience-a
ward in our

family with
no-possible-

daily-receiver
s has been re

named "enthu
siasm breeds

continuous-
expectat

ions".

Do these

early spring
branches ap

pear even
more thinly

exposed be
cause of our

budding-de
sires for

greened-
promising

s.

Does this

daily thirst-
for-newly-

perspective
d-words in any

way resemble
how it feel

s in the
desert with

out rock-sha
dowing-protec

tion.

After those

lost 50 days
and nights do

that always–
impending-dark

ness imaginat
ion begins

to replace
the moon's wit

nessing-ef
fect

s.

Discoverie

s Major

past discover
ies as Nielsen'

s 4th (1916) at
15 or 16 Zelenka'

s master
pieces radio-

wise over a
decade ago

not to forget
Cherubini's

early masses
motivates me

time and a
gain to redis

cover sunken-
treasures

somewhere
in my own

oceaned-depth
s.

Those Seliger

                    masterpiece
                    s now awar

                    ing-me head-
                    on reactivat

                    ing not only past
                    awakening

                    s but here
                    and now

                    dialoguing
                    for-future-

                    appraisal
                    s.

The return

                    of migrating
                    birds heaven

                    s me to re
                    discovered

                    open-space-
                    perspect

                    ive
                    s.

Are my 3

physiothera
pists also

becoming (
each in his

own way) my
pupils as

well Buber
called it

"the life
of a dia

logue".

Freddy

not like
those Mark

Twain early–
jumpers but

more like
those leaf

(not leap
frog's) contem

plative fu
ture–apprais

als.

Those newly-

opened-tulips
dancing a

bout in-all-
possible-dir

ections as
if in need of

a newly-con
ceived-orch

estrat
ion.

I've become

for Freddy
my physiother

apist more
like a double-

fugue Zelenka
or Mozart-like

He's getting
me back in-

balance again
while I'm un

balancing his
well-learned

school-Eng
lish.

It's become

difficult-
for-me to i

magine any
one in-his-

right-eyes
witnessing my

Rosemarie in
her closely-fit

daily appear
ance without

desiring all
of her still

84-year-old
enticing-ap

pearance.

Any teach

er (however
old and ex

perienced)
who doesn't

daily learn
from his

students
should be

sent back for
more "school

ing".

Some person

s remain quite
capable of

making-up
stories or e

ven in just
need for creat

ing entirely-new-one
s Mark Twain

himself remain
ed a story-

book-kind-of-
person.

Imitation

Raphael my
handicapp

ed son now
adult who

seemed to
most especial

ly noticed
my pale-sickly-

look the bald
headedness

In time I be
came an imitat

ion of what
he envision

ed there
and then.

Are we

artists the
best judge of

our own work
I doubt it be

cause words
and ideas

come to me
not from me

forming
their own

sense of be
ing what they

also independ
ently remain

Hindemith for
example as a

conductor of
his own work

s rarely satis
fied my unful

filled-expectat
ions.

Good craftsman

by their very-
raison-d'être

create high
standards That

19th Century
Beethovenian-

Wagnerian
sense-for-gen

ius more a
projection of

ideas-of-their-own-
grandeur.

Do migrat

ing birds
mountain

those pre-
assuming

heights
faster than

their indigen
ous resolve

for home-re
turning nest

ing-right
s.

Initiate

Is spring

first in the
air and then

more notice
ably ground-

based dotted
and clustered

for beautify
ing-pleasure

s.

The lasting remin

der Recovering

from my fa
ther's most

life-threaten
ing illness

the first
taste of fresh

ly-squeezed-
orange-juice

remained that
lasting-re-

minder.

Manfred

you are and
most likely

will always
remain a

church poet and
singer An import

ant one espec
ially for the

1970s A kind
of Paul Gerhardt

I am and will
always remain

a Christian
poet as a Jew

even as a min
ister somewhat

remote (distant)
from church–

domains We're
both unusual

in our own way
but will always

remain other
wise as Paul

Gerhardt and
my Gryphius.

The "Naming

of things" as
they really

are a primary
concern of a

genuine poet
Yet we name

them with our
own (quite de

decipherable)
initial

s.

We Jews

and Ukrainian
s share a

common heritage
Ours is the

INRI we've never
deserved lived-

up-to Their's
a nation (Yes

a holy one)
that has never

become their
own.

Scholar

ship has al
ways sailed

a pre-routed
pre-determin

ing course
Genuine art

pursues its
own most per

sonal (if at
times even

less) self-con
fiding way

s.

Returning

birds in un
endless

ly-samed-
flocks yet

as the popu
lar song

"for each
his own".

February

24 that sin
gular day

that once
again ended

the endless
"peace for

our time
s".

Yes Flor

ian a day
without a

single poem
as soundless

as the o
cean's

bottom
less-depth.

Don't e

ver record
what I (at

the height
of my power

s) failed
to express.

"For my own

good" What
good hers

or when the
words (as

my father
once reveal

ed at my birth)
failed–him.

In-becoming

This day's

still in-be
coming

whatever it
will form

but outside
my momentary

word–span.

Manfred

these have
become more

or less
yours for–

you Bundle
them up

the "Manfred
poems" of

February
21st/22nd.

Yes Chung

a lesser
world (but

just as in
timate)

A world
that cease

s to be
ours while

being pre
pared for

what's not
yet fully–

becoming.

Only a per

sonal God
can fully-

heal Only
a living

wife can
help replace

the imper
sonal-every

day.

Phantom

ed secrets

can never
remain al

ways-kept
sealed-up

at first
unnamed

but then
in the depth

of night's
unknown re

sponding-
voice.

Had it

actually
happen

ed this
way or that

Can face
remain two-

faced at
night at day

turned-on
and then

(when necess
ary) off.

Hebrew

a language
never-act

ually-learn
ed but

neverthe
less reveal

ing his true
(if-forsak

en)-identity.

Was that

opera's text
written by

a Pole and/
or a Jew

but it re
mained for

Weinberg
at his heart'

s depth both
to reveal

its true–
atonal–na

ture.

Phantom

ed Only
after those

50 days
and nights

of self-de
ception

(when it be
came necess

ary to
sleep alone

down-stair
s to that

house's
once origin

ed phantom
ed-intent

ions A
voice

(at first
foreign to

his ears)
took-on

the form
of its

(his own)
actual-ori

gins.

Neverthe

less a Jew–
free Germany

to the very
depth of

its blood–
spelled in

tention
s.

Epilogue

It remain
ed finally

self-certain
ed Her

grave-stone
close-by

eternal
ly-his.

The way Marc

Chagall's eyes
expanded and

hands grasped
for a fully breas

ted-woman
somehow remind

ed me of my
father just

sizing-up the
Thanksgiving

turkey for its
first juicy

thrust through.

Do those paint

ers too sensual
ly oriented

as Renoir and
even Rubens

often lack
the concentrat

ion of a justi
fied–spiritual–

intent.

Florian not

only nominal
father of an

extended family–
tree while in

timately in
his–own–parti

cular right–
of–way for

additional–
even physiothera

peutic explorat
ions.

A late Febru

ary sun-down
shadowing

its own with
holding-in

tentions
for a

still cold-
embracing-

night.

Sensing her

Swabian
anti-Pietist

ic-inclinat
ions I Luther

ised once again
his "alone

through God's
grace" and the

ultimate
good works of

His Crucifix
ion and Resur

rection.

When culture

(even on vacat
ions) comes

too short she
even begins

to question
the length of

her past-
shadowing

s.

When the

poetic-ten
sion still

remains unre
solved the

impending
word-flow

still called-
upon for its

continuing-
rhythmic–im

pulsing
s.

Refreshingly otherwise

Such yearly

or bi-yearly
conversat

ions rarely
touched unin

habited-depth
s but they

still proved
refreshing

ly-other
wise.

At the

very least
they inhabit

ed past-
times with

"I haven't
thought about

that before."

Fasching

(Mardi Gras
in New Orlean

s) awakens
(almost before

hand) historic
religious person

al and other
still self–

activating
pre–concept

ions That a
lone's good

reason for
its imaginat

ive (if
at chosen–

times) danger
ous dream–

calling
s.

Call it old

fashioned
He quite

surprised
when his

daughter's
suitor asked

him for her
own hand

neither of
which held-

behind from
viewing-sake.

Out-dated

The snow-

drops seemed
quickly out-

dated in the
immensing of

blooming-ex
pectation

s.

Open-ended

After your

once athlet
ic balance

has unbalanc
ed even your

daily step-a
surety each

outside walk
seems unassur

edly open-
ended.

I never

would have ex
pected her

to well-u
pon the quality

of Seliger's
late works

Even Uncultur
ed Pietistic

Malmsheim con
tinues to offer-

up new-surprise
s.

The New Freedom

We're now in
joyous-accord

with the new
freedom from

family freedom
from faith and

religion freedom
most of all from

our-self Freedom
for loneliness

es' free-reign.

When common-decen

cy becomes so

decently common
that it

ceases to ful
fill its origin

al urgency The
same remains

true of a
language that

fails to con
vey a genuine-

expressive
ness.

He finally

escaped from
that other

wise reign of
sickness

and hospital-
attendance

that re-formed
his most daily

self-assurance
But once

freed of
routine robbed

of personal
freedom he

could hardly i
magine its fully

acceptable-
return.

Border-line

They finally
decided to

call it (in a
less self-assur

ing way) border-
line but could

hardly agree on
its scholar

ly acceptable
borders between

what and that
supposedly o

ther end.

Life-time border

s Each post-

sickness-
walk had be

come as a re
establishing

of newly
sensed and

achieved life-
time borders

as his 7 or 8
year-old ones

between Oak
Lane Brite

Avenue and
the still dis

stant range
of his ele

mentary school-
time appearan

ces.

After thos

50 sickness-
lost-days

he felt in
wardly the

need to re
gain his

loved-ones
sexually-ac

ceptable-com
petence.

Identity-Cause

It remained

that daily
poetry-access

to the once-
establish

ed-person
he'd left so

unidentifi
ably-behind.

Still suspi

cious of
each and e

very man that
looked that

way at his
still desirable

wife he began
to wonder if

Shakespeare'
s Othello hadn't

been penned
most personal

ly that uneasy-
way.

The creative

urge may be
reduced in

a half–accepta
ble way to

sexual desire
certaining

of personal
experience

an aesthet
ic freedom–

find or what
ever of its

own pre-
determining

s.

He kept say

ing to his
usually-uneasy-

say it all
before the

stage becomes
finally cleared

of all its
left-over de

bris and the
curtain's ulti

mately closed-
down.

Is artistic

creativity
nothing more

or less than
a life-time

detective
urge for dis

covering those
hardly marked

steps left
even self-

indulgent
ly behind.

Were those

so come-on
eyes used

partly
disclos

ing the dark
ly enticing

pleasures
well below

their surfac
ing-claim

s.

To take

possession
of a woman

a wife it
must become

all-inclusive
fully-packed

but don't for
get to hold

it daily
tightly-

dear.

A lovely

and faithful wo
man's well-

worthy of a
life-time

investment
The other type

(more common
these days) can

be bought and
sold at a

daily exchange-
rate.

Keeping-up

with your
daily poetic-

output's
more like chas

ing stray dogs
(even those

street one
s) over time'

s always-ex
panding-field-

length.

Last time

our secondary
physiothera

pist came with
a full-length

stretcher If
he tries that a

gain I'll kindly
aware him

of the clos
est route to

our accompany
ing-grave

yard.

Advice for

a teenage-
youngster

Don't ever a
gain be taken-

in by the inno
cent look may

lead you unaware

d down those
darkest-alley-

ways.

Night phant

oms Sleep

left him
restless

ly-alone
as those

night phantom
s descended

upon his
most imagin

ary fears feed
ing on the

crumbs of
a scarcely-in

habited-past.

His twice

unscheduled
Hades visit

left him pain
fully silent

shadowing
a world that

wouldn't be
come re-awaken

ed.

Felix the

under-taker
will most like

ly not in
dulge in that

ultimate
under-taking

but he's week
ly helping

me reestablish
a new ground-

surfacing-
appeal.

His mother

as sculptress
and designer

of mainly house-
hold arti

cles reawakens (at
least in me)

that old and
ever-present

Chinese-Japan
ese what's pure

art and what's
its decorative

side-affects
Can they uni

fy a whole
ness.

Other-timed *(for Andreas)*

I wouldn't
want to live

in France
where abortion

may become an
unalienable-

right and so-
called homo-

phobia more
like criminal-

intent.

From my educative-past (8)

a) What social

scientists
must learn

is that philo
sophic–continu

ity hardly
should remain

as a lasting
criteria for

depth and
quality.

b) Such art

ists as Modigli
ani remain eas

ily identifi
able doesn't

guarantee
for quality

or even orig
inality.

c) Some artists

as Picasso al
ways remain com

petent at
showing-off

their "new
style" Braque'

s sameness never
theless (dis

pite its re
petitiveness)

still remains
for me more-

personal
ly-genuine.

d) Some artist

s as the sym
phonist Niel

sen remain
always that

Others as
Carissimi

a one-work
greatness

Despite his
genius Haydn

still enabled
to compose

first-rate
concerti a

discipline
that rarely

endeared to
his form-

enveloping-
expressive

ness.

e) Beethoven'

s essential
dependence

on his "mas
ter" Haydn

not only
obvious

through the
forms they

favored and de
veloped from

birth to per
fection.

f) Genuine

Pan-Slavs as
Dostoyevsky

and Solzhenitsyn
remained deep

ly convinced and
convincing Christ

ions Should we
fully accept

one-side of
their self-in

tegrating-
person while

rejecting
the other.

g) Was the tradit

ional French
canonisation

of Aristotle
s' dramatic

theorys singular
ly self–ordain

ing and/or an ob
stacle against

future even
Shakespear

ian–insight
s.

h) Is it legiti

mate to use
a nation's

past history
(as is often

done) to
sanctify pre

sent–day poli
cies.

Feeling

like new-found-
lovers once

again after a
long respite

in the 62nd
year of lov

ing-her-back
to the momen

tary-now.

A fully

hearty "Eng
lish breakfast"

Some softly
self-express

ing-kisses
and I begin

to feel once
again the

blood rising
for peak-per

formance
s.

The snow

late but still
self-decisive

has decided to
stay-on for

a weekend of
keeping-close-

together
ness.

At 85

It becomes
difficult
to actualise

the daily
news especial

ly future-ex
pectation

s will it re

main ours
or simply

leaving-us-
left-behind

ers.

Einstein

ian Living from

day to day
(or is it do

ing that with
us) No matter

time has
re-dis

covered its
own measur

ing-rod.

Middling-things-

out Transition

al times as
late-February

to mid–April
more like

that children'
s game one

step forward
s two backward

s Whereas I
seem once a

gain to be
middling–

things-out.

Too many

economic dang
er-signs in

China India
even here in

Germany After
my long recov

ery it's not
become a time

for worrying
"What will

be will be".

For the

first time
in weeks

it snowed
in the night

a light snow
hardly express

ive of any
thing deeper

Was it meant
to cover over

a light but
long-past-

guilt Or did
it speak on-

its-own-right
a purity of

self-sanctifi
cation.

Who is to

judge of other'
s misdeed

s before re
conciling his

own and who
can guarantee

a satisfying
forgiveness.

He wouldn'

t recognise
his own sickly

father perhaps
because he'd al

ways been that
way since

birth and need
ed a strongly-

imaged-father
He turned-aside

not a word
between them.

If the imagin

ed-woman can
never fully

realise the
actual-one

which must
change to

accord a
genuine to

gether
ness.

Florian

realised that
some words

which had
lost their

up-to-date
American

flavor
could be re

established
in-their-own-

right if
only in a

less-transform
ed-English.

Falling-in-

love or fall

ing-asleep
both off-

balancing
one's own

self-certain
ing raison-

d'être.

With Rose

marie and my
self the communi

cation's so
confused like

the quarter
back calling

for a long
pass and re

ceiving an
end-around in

its more
ground-based

down-to-
earthi

ness.

Out in the dark

True enough

my hearing's
at times self-

routed and
the ears not

fully cleans
ed for an

adequate-re
ceptivity

whereas she
continues to

leave me out-
in-the-dark

of the exact
who what

when where
s.

Coca Cola

may "hit the
spot" and

Pepsi pep-
you-up at

least moment
arily they

seem to satis
fy your own

up-lifting
needs.

A quiet

late winter

afternoon
If one listen

s hard enough
the birds seem

to leave their
footsteps

barely-touch
ed for snow

and the self–
withholding

sky's watching–
out as if we'

ve forgotten
to(o).

Phantomed

If you can

no longer
recognise

yourself
in the mirror

It could be
those 50 lost

days and
nights will

continue
to phantom

your own
self-being.

On Mardi Gras

Neil dreamt
for the first

time in his
life he'd be

come a killer
Children

just love ex
changeable

self-person
s but many

realise even
that playing–

with-fire can
burn-you-right–

through.

If I no long

er trust what
once had be

come him
self Should I

then trust
that mirror

ed–otherwise–
self.

If as Calder

ón and
supposed Haydn

"Life's but
a dream" Do

we ever real
ly wake-up.

If as

Stevens imag
ined 3 black

birds can be
come involv

ed in what
's involving

even more
than my own

self-assur
ity.

Ghosted

If what

changes be
cause it's

envisioned
through o

ther eyes
and sense

s Has this
post-Heisen

berg-world
become but a

ghost-of-
itself.

If the Good

Lord created
us as a whole

and in the
image of Him

self then
each operat

ion (however
minor it might

seem at first)
endangers the

unity of our
(His) whole-be

ing.

Lady Chatterley

The line's bet

not really bet
ween "love and

fascination"
But the moon-

tidal-flow
of sensual

ity's-uninhib
ited-desir

ings.

If as modern

science contin

ually proves
our senses as

a false guide
for "what real

ly is" then
shouldn't we

old-fashion
ed-Christian

s continue to
reserve a spec

ial-place for
our too-lesser-

used-Bible

"What actual

ly happen
ed" the

key histori
cal (Rank

ean) quest
ion of his

student days
Haunted

him not
only those

50 lost
days and

(even more
important)

night
s.

Must the

past become
clarified

while accept
ing the on

coming future
or can it

remain at
a kind

of limbo
ed perpet

ually unre
solving Ha

des.

His life

now more
or less

divided
in the u

sual three
past present

future
but remain

ing unresolv
ed with

its actual
then and there

here and
now.

Always

As an histor

ian Only Now
in that 50

day dilemma
of personal

history did
he fully under

stand while
he'd always

been an
historian

pre-and past
scholarly

as well.

Downstair

s how after
those 50

days and
nights rele

gated to
the more

accessible
downstair

s foreign
from the

continuing
steps of

his histori
cal mystery.

It snowed

again last
night This

time a bit
heavier cov

ering–over
more deeply

his search
for those

"real" days
and night

s.

Downstairs

otherwise
perspectiv

ed with those
long-ago-

books and re
cords Those

pre–50–days
documented

to their his
torical long-

ago know-
how.

Aunt Sylvia'

s advice (my not-
so-favoured

Aunt Sylvia) in
a somewhat

Polonius–like
manner "David

you should
marry a beauti

ful woman" After
noting that

such a woman re
main followed

by men's desir
ing eyes I'm

not so certain
her advice

was well
thought–out.

Why is it

that certain
rooms contin

ue to haunt
us like where

I was treated
those 50 days

and especially
night

s still at a
live as the

living-truth-
itself.

German painter

ly-expression

ism (especial
ly the more

Northern vin
tage) usually

turns–me–
off Somehow

despite their
mostly pre

vailing anti–
Nazi bias

employing a
kind of "aes

thetic lang
uage" close-

to-the-time
s Nolde

"Blood and
Earth" painter

as anti-semit
ic Nazi

neverthe
less never-

accepted-by-
them.

Holy

That once
sense-of-holi

ness now largely
secularised

still lives-
on Hasn't sex

ual culminat
ion taken-on

an almost Holy
Communion

ethos For some
it's a foot

ball team for o
thers an a

dored actress
I've once ex

perienced a
friend whose

family (now
mostly dead)

has remained
holy for her.

This interim

time late Febru
ary to mid–

April reminds
me of persons

future-orient
ed while still

past-inhabit
ing whereas

my time's in
terimed through

those lost 50
days and espec

ially night
s.

I'm also in

terimed between

my faithful
priestly years

and the poet
who's reem

erged from the
Hades of accumulat

ing-silences
Which person

which way interimed
by those 50 speech

less days and
nights.

Change-of-

landscape's
change-of-

themes the win
ter has involved

me once again
in its time–

holding if purify
ing presence.

As much of

the interior Uk
raine remains

untouched by this
"total war" so

did Rosemarie'
s remote house

and extended
garden offer a

war–refuge
for her fanta

sied–soul.

Priviledged-pro

tected The

two-of-us
have remained

privileg
ed-protected

in these time
s of self-

destruction
Protected as

well from the
inner urgings

of such rest
less-time

s.

Does the

truth establish
a higher level

of understand
ing as the

beautified
self-delus

ions of my
memoired-

past.

Being watch

ed If you know
you're being

watched (as
many today)

does it help to
protect your

own wishful-
thinking.

It snowed

him in
to those irretriev

able realms
of his past-

history.

One can't

make-up for
terrible mis

deeds with
beautifully

conceived New
Year's resolut

ions.

Holding-back

(He held–

back) knowing
it was per

haps better
not to real

ise the irre
parable coming

damage for
mind and

soul.

False imagin

ings can destroy
the foundation

s of real life
This new fallen

snow must settle-
down to the

realms of my
inner-being.

The earlier

> more imaginat
> ive finely-
>
> sensed at
> times child-
>
> like Klee I far
> prefer to much
>
> of his abstract
> schematic
>
> later work.

However close

I may feel
personally to

them when
Jesus the Bible

and our parish
remain the

only relevant
themes I begin

to feel my
self growing

smaller as
through a mag

ic-potent
and the wond

rous world
of The Creat

ion and of
culture as

well.

Macke

happily marr

ied to a beaut
ful woman full

of humour and
adventurous

spirit A natur
al one might

say but if he
hadn't died so

early at 28 in
The Great War

would he
have remained

so even ripen
ed during the

most diffi
cult years

of the 20s
30s and

40s.

Kandinsky

must have
been an off-

centered
kind of per

son because
most all of

his painting
s leave

me center
less as well.

It may be

caused by my
own personal

and cultural
limitation

s but I fail
to find real

depthed–great
ness in the

best known wo
men composer

s and painter
s while the

novel and
poetry is quite

another
thing But

where are
truly great

women dra
matist

s.

For Rosemarie

At 85

Desiring you'
s more than

my eyes
and lips

could possi
bly express

You have be
come more for

me than my-
entire-being

and all the
more than erotic

words could
fully realise.

Why can't

we begin again
Even time's

lost its own
continuity

We'll embrace
it again

the origins
of our very-

being.

The Garden

of Youth re
mained no

wheres to
be discover

ed in Florida'
s tropical climb

s we shall to
its very un

timely-peak
s.

Why must so

many Christ

ians divide
between cul

ture and faith
The whole

world's fill
ed with His

creative-
word of

the prophets
the poets

glorifying
His very-

being.

Putin the

czar with
all that im

perial-pres
tige Putin

the Pan-slav
still mapped

with blood-
historical

esteem.

Cancelling

It might

seem relevant
for some to

cancel cult
ure and its

historical
by-paths

while ultimate
cancelling

their
own personal

raison d'ê
tre.

Unforget

table The "Unfor

gettable Allan"
would have us

forget that he
never once

called while
Neil steered

through a
10 hour

snowstorm e
ven without

winter-tire
s.

I remapped-

her-out hands–
over-lips much

as Columbus re
conceived A

merica's ar
chaic-pre

sence.

Poem

ing's a very

selective
process

like choosing
a girl-friend

it must all
sense-together

the lithely ex
pressive body

with its dips
and seductive

curves all
well-spaced for

a receptive
response.

Women's

Some clothing'

s meant as a
personal dis

playing as an
ice-cream's

topping's es
pecial flavour

ings and color-
enchantment

s Others sens
ing as well

thorough
fares to a

most self-satisfy
ing destina

tion.

A woman-

in-love only
fully realise

s her bodily-
enchantment

s when touch
ed and kiss

ed to their
awakened-

flavor
ings.

Does promis

cuity help
discover the

many-sided
person or

does it re
sult in a

confusion
of one's own

raison-d'être.

22

22 always

revealed my
home-stay-

belonging
My mother's

as well Have
some family

tradition
s become so

aspired-
that-way.

Has the pre

sent–day–cult–
of–other–sex

ualities
become another

means of deny
ing The Good

Lord's own creat
ive certify

ings.

"We (I)

shall return"
not only Gener

al MacArthur'
s verdict o

ver the Philip
pines but an

aging lover'
s vacated 50

lost days and
especially

nights from
his still ar

dently ripen
ed lady.

Winced

as a phan

tomed in
sinuation

She winced
when I exact

ly described
what could-

have-been in
recognition

of her supposed guilt or
as a means

of expressing
her personal-dis

gust or possibly-
both.

Quick forget

ters as quick
forgivers hard

ly realise
that past his

tory's not only
permanently

remembered
beyond one'

s own time-
lengths.

Does each

generation
make its

own fresh-
start or is

each becoming
an unwritten

chapter in
a book not-

yet-fully
bound.

Some feel

(as Neil once
said) we'll

(all) go up
to a heaven of

our long-ex
pectant-par

ents.

Most German

s today re
main little

concerned
with death'

s own pre–
inhabiting

concern
s as if life

remained no
one else's

than their
own time-sus

pending
s.

If preacher

s learned first
to preach to

themselves
then the oft

highly-placed-
pulpit would

have to be lower
ed more than

even a notch-
or-two.

"Also rises"

Even the

snow "also
rises" through

the darken
ed depth of

my time-tell
ing recollect

ions.

Only later

(perhaps

best so)
we realised

we were
playing the

same game
Some call it

soccer the
other foot

ball or
was it

really the
same game.

Fully-prepared

When Miss

Blackburn
cleaned-off

the 2nd grade
blackboard

we felt fully
prepared for

a freshly-
conceived-

new-start.

The belated

return of win
ter senses much-

of-the-same
almost void

of movement
it helps si

lence a dis
tancing past.

Can there

realise a
fresh new

start at a
common 85

"Never too
late" they

say what's
actually real

ising its
own-apparent-

truth.

4 clocks

each on the
4 sides of

the same room
Each of differ

ent sizes and
make-ups Each

differently
aged I guess

that's the way
our family

life must
have appear

ed even when
the time wasn't

quite-the-
same.

Biblical

history's
the story

(or dialogue
if you will)

of The Good
Lord's educat

ion of his
own child

ren.

Florian'

s brother
dead in his

early 20s
continued
to reappear

to Florian
through

his night-
time presen

ce years-on-
end Was that

only dream.

Susanna

's Elders bath
ed-viewed Wall

ace Stevens
almost in

to poetic ec
tasy and Veron

ese in to a
curious extra-

touch and side-
view special-

lock Who will
doubt woman'

s naked-fas
cination even

(or especial
ly) for a

ging men.

1975

Was 1975 In
the Glass of

Winter then
As One the

Elisabeth
Press the turning–

point in my
poetry now

crisply–conden
sed classical

ly–clear Or
has the sensitiv

ity to words
persons

and feeling
s remained

much–the–same.

This late

bare–minded
winter–cold

has undress
ed some of

the warmth of
my previous

feelinged–
nearness.

As Florian's feel

ings for his bro
ther's loss

less intensely
so are these

50 Day and
Night Phantom

s fading in
to an irrecon

cilable past.

Why have

Buster Keaton
and Alec Guin

ness become
lost names for

Freddy age 25
Because they've

become dated even
land and time

ly and/or be
cause their

humour has
staled.

Long-length

ed Once the
snow's become

long-lengthed
even in late

February
keeps you

down as well
ground-bas

ed.

For Florian

Even simply
appearance

s may appear
otherwise

perspectiv
ed if worded

in to their
special-singu

larity.

Those 50

long days and
especially

nights would
take possess

ion of my
very-being deny

ing their ex
clusive demand

s of a phan
tomed-over

wiseness.

Middled

Dream or
reality the

ground-based
every day'

s a duality
between imagina

tion and act
ual time-call

ings While I
and Poem caught-

in-the-middle
of a word-

controlling-
aesthetic.

Redefining

If The Good
Lord's creat

ion's word-
based then

its actual
callings in

the prophetic
word's rede

fining-sensi
bility.

Even at

25 Freddy real
ises the life-

preserving-
necessity

of fear's
own most en

compassing
(if self-

limited) claim
s.

For most

> life's unsub
> stancial rai
>
> son-d'être
> (actually
>
> our own)
> dies with
>
> our 5-acted
> curtained-
>
> down.

Swiss choco

> late-almonded
> A "minor" fall
>
> after those
> 50 lost days
>
> and nights
> left me once
>
> again off-bal
> anced the liv
>
> ing room floor
> stained with
>
> the blood of
> that past
>
> night's insuf
> ficient claims
>
> on my chocolate-
> almonded well-
>
> being.

Sleep's

become an in
terlude of

its own self-
calling "knitt

ing-up the ra
velled cares

of day" or
haunting an

irreconcil
able-past.

While time'

s either mak
ing-the-most

of my limited
self-establish

ing-resour
ces or secur

ing a less-
than-permanent-

hold on each
day's self-re

claiming-auton
omy.

Freddy's

young dog lick
ed his master'

s fully-expend
ing day back in

to its contin
ual life-call

ings Dogs may
understand

but in a lang
uage of their

own instinct
ual-raison-

d'être.

My 3 young

weekly thera
pists Florian

Freddy and
my faithful

pall-bearer
daily reestab

lishing my
body's life-

claims Each of
them life and

help-oriented
not essential

ly (as perhaps
most youths

today) money-
minded.

Ours has be

come with my 3
helpers a trans

itional-dialog
ue of generat

ions of exper
ience and of

life-assuming
otherwise-ex

pectation
s.

Emeritus

While he re
mains not al

ways in the
background

as a teacher
and minister-

Emeritus
prompted

anew
by their youth

ful-impetus.

Life-essential

Each four-of-
us women in

the background
most unseen

but neverthe
less life-es

sential.

Washer-women

biblically
from Babylon

or modern
painterly

Van Gogh Here
day by day wo

men mostly
in their 50s

divorced main
ly from the Bal

kans keep clean
ing me from

head-to-toe
St. Peter-like.

Many-faced

At our age
after those

50 lost day
s and night

s sleep good
eats being

the repetitive
temptation

s of a life
similar to

my highly-
spoiled-youth

while I write
each-day-

through and
love as much as

I can Lost time'
s many-faced

as well.

Another of

those cold Feb
ruary morning

s Even the
picked-pretty-

flowers seem
resistant to

its silently
embracing urge

The stars have
left their

traditional
witnessing-

rights-be
hind.

Even our

children and
grandchild

ren have no
real need of

our house
Little person

al response
when Munich's

fine cultural
life (that doesn'

t interest them)
and the vacation

lakes and moun
tains within e

qual-radius.

The time of

return to nor
mal behavior

(whatever that
may mean)

And I unable
to takeover

as in the
past house-re

sponsibilit
ies I feel a

bit left-out
of this daily

raison d'être
left over (es

pecially at
night) to The

Phantom's dia
bolical-in

sinuation
s.

Our famil

iar intimate
world's

as Lenore'
s lessen

ing from
year to year

yet enabled
to replenish

with more
youthful

growth the
senility of

age I write
we love each

day into our
own time-call

ings.

Love-Sickness

First time
in a long

while I've
seen Rosemarie

laugh wheth
er our good

doctor treat
s love-sick

ness as well
He full of

Bavarian
beer-uprising-

spirits kept an
exception

al poker-face
caused per

haps from Cor
ona's reacti

vating claim
s.

Black lives

do matter even

those chained
and bound by

their own peo
ple for the

cotton fields
of the Ameri

can South And
what do we

say about Hannah
Arendt and those

Jewish middle-
men listing

names and
addresses of

their own peo
ple for Himm

ler's death-
crew Our life

only matter
s if their-

s-do-as-
well.

Do we with

sisters older
or younger

have a better
chance of a

good marriage
knowing the

whims and
wiles of the o

ther sex at–
first-hand.

Unrhymed

Who's to
rhyme-togeth

er the fra
gile-tenacity

of the ear
liest-spring-

flowers of
the gentle

lithe-birch
and their Nor

thern Canadian
heartiness.

Shell Island

On the look-
out Sanibel

shell–island
gracing the

tropical time-
flow with its

delicate
time-touched

coloring
s.

Rosemarie'

s blued this
room in to

her color-
instinctual–

finds My hands
and lips sensu

ally-prepared–
as–well.

Re-birthed

A once call
ed "Pietist

ic minister"
composing

erotic love-
poems for his

wife's lips
and other en

ticing part
s nearing her

85th time-
telling re-

birthed-day.

He wasn't

sufficient
ly prepared

as Traudl
with her color

ed-bird-
book as that

strange majest
ically-beauti

fying bird
landed for

but a soli
tary branched-

moment on his
mid-afternoon

imagining
s.

Operation

s are never
a-routine-mat

ter They're
lots of bac

teria waiting
just for you

in the hospital
and The Good

Lord may not
take-it look

ing-aside as
you undo His

finalised-work
ings While some

remain plagued
by those Phantom

ed-Spirits Oper
ations are

never a rou
tine matter.

Unexplain

able F. Scott
Fitzgerald

from charact
er taste and

initial artis
tic make-up

a lower-level
writer of in

ferior time
s Yet his

late works (es
pecially Gats

by) display a
poetic and per

sonal sensibil
ity of the

highest order
What or who'

s to explain
this extreme

ly-contradict
ory-person.

Hemingway'

s muscle-mas
culinity com

bined with a
(but singular

exception)
inability to

understand
woman's sensi

bility still
developed a

modern Ameri
can way of

literary-ex
pressive

ness.

Willa Cather

at her sensitive-
best My Anton

ia and A Lost
Lady displays

a highly per
sonal means of

expression
lesser known

because of
her transit

ional linguist
ic mean bet

ween a dying
romanticism

and a not
quite

modern-ling
guistic-com

pressive
ness.

When and

whom if ever
completely e

mancipated
the American

novel from its
lasting depend

ence on the
English Great

"Tradition".

Are Henry

James and T. S.
Eliot simply

lost voice
d European-

American-out
siders.

Re-birthed

Do my mid–
80 poetic-e

rotic love
poems defy

(in part)
physical real

ity or have
they become

expressive
of an inher

ent rebirth
of personal–

linguistic-
distinct

ion.

Does American

frontier Mani
fest Destiny

especially
invoked by

the Louisiana
Purchase

or is it in
herently pre

sent in the
indigenous

landscape-
schooling

s.

"Kindred

Spirits" (I'
ve several

of those)
they used-to-

call the sin
gularity

of a mind
and heart's un

known yet
commonly

sourced even
pre-histori

cal-together
ness.

Timeless

ness When
spring has

early prepar
ed its ground–

based–color
ing–appearan

ce The return
of winter'

s in
sistence

on its (my)
time at the

threshold of
death's clos

ed–door time
lessness.

Lover'

s hand–hold
ing insinua

tes warmth
bestowed

with foreign
breath–claim

ings.

Recycling

50,000 and
more dead-bur

ied in the
earthquake'

s rubble lit
tle to differ

entiate from
the after-

match of pre-
timed expecta

tions Histori
cal recycling

once-again.

Otherwised

We've little
to learn

from our par
ent's other

wise experien
ces time and

personally
remote-from-

our-own.

Chronical

ed Why chroni

cle the past
writing-us-

up in a more
detailed and

less significant
ly-assumed-

way.

Only the

two-of-us
a world round

ed in to a
post-Colum

bian univer
se.

The 12ᵗʰ

grade pauses
at Scarsdale

High School
felt him lost

while ocean
ing impersonal

grammatical-
abstract

ions.

Taking-side

s Must one
take side

s if they
both remain

out–of–bound
s of my off–

sided Jewish-in
heritance.

A tiny vase

with sprinkled
snow drops

inhabiting
my loved one'

s morning-
expressive

ness I also
feel flower

ed for a morn
ing-refrain.

Hanging lamp

s down to an
expectant-

presence
answered by

a thinly time-
lengthening-

response.

Rampaged

Call it a
rampage not

of the bull-
running-

kind but of
poems 100

plus in 3
days Not to

be held-back
from their

pre-designing
time-hold

s.

Jealousy

How can one
look Othello-

like at Rose
marie's (e

ven at 85)
blossoming-

beauty with
out an aware

ness look for
others doing

much-the-
same.

Some say

the right
thing in the

wrong-way
Others the

wrong thing
in just the

right-kind-
of-way re

minding once
again of the

Latzel Bro
thers.

A genuine

Catholic-soul
ed-Bavarian

who's lost
his taste for

beer must also
be question

ing his own
raison d'être.

Some artists

as Degas Cézanne
and Monet I

often admire
for these or

those reason
s but mostly fail to

affect me deep
ly-existent

ially.

Only when

the moon become
s voiced once-

again does
one realise

it sustain
ed-rhythmic-

impulsing
s.

Feeling as

hamed of one'
s own suspic

ions answer
ing those

self-shadow
ing back–

into–the–
night–wind'

s transpar
ently–escap

ing.

Name-dropp

ing The repeat
ed use of

name-dropping
a puppy-dog

attempt at a
once-expect

ed–bigness.

Familiar

ity's the
ease of a

momentary
timeless

ness.

European

squirrels
small and

lithely plea
sed for nut-

swelling in
stinctual-

phrasing
s.

My eldest

sister Doris
(bless her

memory)
read almost

all the books
in her high

ly-educated-
shelves While

I completed
those empty

spaces of
mine with the

bound-words
of my own-de

fining
s.

Dressing

s for salad
s as for

not quite-
self-satisfy

ing women
attracts exo

tic-impuls
ings.

Retelling

the-past a
never possi

ble endless
two-way ven

ture.

College

at my elder
sister's

time remained
a kind of

marriage-mar
ket 4 years

for a life-
long-prepara

tion.

Cleansing'

s With Shakes
peare's drama

s one gener
ation lies

with its blood-
stained past

while another
partially-pre

pared for-its-
future-role

Who cleansed
that violent

ly–appropri
ated–stage.

Death-offer

ing These in
sects instin

cted with
spring's flut

tering de
signs of a

temporary
flight–appeal

soon died for
winter's return

ing death-off
ering

s.

Butterflies

If there'
s an artist

ic red-line
between the

decorative
and lyrical

as with Mat
isse prefigur

ed on both
sides Where

do those
early-bird-

butterflies
distinguish

their fligh
ty presence.

The Latzel Bro

thers two-side
s of a blue-

ribbon church-
cut The one

distinguish
edly time-ap

parent the o
ther caused

with a primitive
ly-eternal-

mouthed-truth.

Blood-recall

ings Pain's in
cisive-voice

reclaimed e
ven the once

curtained
routes while

now blood-re
calling

s.

Reminding

again of Strind
berg's hurting–

the–most
woman of

his loving–
claim

s.

A soothing

most–necess
ary–sleep

now denied
of its rest

ful–need
s while

pained with un
pleasant-re

membrance
s.

The dark

satiated
his timeful-

repose with
fears of a

pre-determin
ing end.

"Why is this

> night differ
> ent from e
>
> very other
> night" be
>
> cause it re
> mains alive
>
> and wakeful
> ly even hurt
>
> fully time–
> consuming.

That moon

> must be
> watching–
>
> through its
> apparently
>
> self–assum
> ing–compos
>
> ure.

This is

the time of
forgotten

misdeeds re
levantly en

compassing
a route of

no-ways-out.

Interlude

s Such inter
ludes pained

with repeat
ed remembran

ces of a
still-unresolv

ing-future.

Self-pity

When self-
pity's be

come the
only access

ible retreat
through

those moun
tains of un

resolving
fears.

He began

to feel like
one of those

unrelated
grave-watch

ers more often
his own

still undaunt
ing ground-

depth.

Pursued

This pain
continue

s to pursue
my body mind

and whatever'
s left of my

once peaceful
ly-intending

quietude
s like a

swiftly-surfa
cing-beast-

of-prey.

None of

those child
hood hide-

outs left to
bypass this

swiftly-on-
coming-pain.

Sleep at

last the
pillowed

ease of pre
vious self-

contentment
s.

Women how

ever innocent
they might

first-appear
still appro

priating
those self-

defensive
hurt-eye-

lengths and
that penetrat

ing-look of
why-did-you-

do-that-to-
me.

With marri

age and sexual–
advisors now

replacing the
priest's once

sanctified–
confession

al–realms
The Good Lord

himself must have
remained shelt

ered from such
continual se

cularised
self–certain

ties.

Blizzard of

'47 After the
New York blizz

ard of '47
I was a young

ster then
when all had

been transform
ed in to a

prolonging-
silenced-

whiteness
and the ab

stract-sky-
scrapers

heralding
a timeless

ly-vacant-
hold.

16th Floor of

Honolulu's
open-windowed

to the Pacif
ic's herald

ing strength
while we litt

led-down to
such sun and

oceaned tide
ful-perspect

ives.

The first

sight of Rose
marie left

me spell-
bound at the

sight of such
a genuinely

modest beauty
become trans

formed in to
a personal

ly express
ive-near

ness.

That Empty

Thursday
One could (re)

call it The
Empty Thurs

day not e
ven a doctor'

s visit or
tomorrow

's pall-bear
ing-thera

pist A day
for itself

windowed-
for-silen

ce.

Momentary

Paradise
My Rosemarie

dressed-in-
blue of an

especially
delicate

ly light-
nature as

the early
spring day

endearing
this dream-

spreading
momentary-

paradise.

Bellini Alt

dorfer Ruisdael

C. D. Frederick
Constable Corot

and Gauguin
my landscap

ists each for
differing rea

sons Bellini'
s classical-

purity Altdorfer
's seclusive

ly pre-Romant
ic Ruisdael's

dark and brood
ingness Frederic and

Constable's christian-
spaceless(full)ness

land-based
wholeness Corot

's poetic-trans
parency and

Gauguin's my
stical primitive-

(re)-awakening
s.

He shouldn't

make the same
mistake as my

legalistic-
liberal uncle's

getting his
wild son time

and again out-
of-trouble un

til he fin
ally-committed-

suicide.

He never openly

admitted his
own mistakes

and even
guilt The

ball was
always in

the other's
court If we

live from for
giveness and

love perhaps
his wife would

stand better-
off when fac

ing his creat
or and redeem

er.

Pitied or

loved At his
age it's eas

ier to be pit
ied than

loved Weakness
and pain are

to be pitied
whereas love

remains a
wholeness

of fullness
permanent-

well-being.

Weathered

One can't
weather-him-

back to
spring to

the gentle
touch of such

first-flower
ing-moment

s yet he can
still blossom

at the sight
of his loved-

one's near
ness.

A new day

to forget the
problems of

the previous
one as subdu

ed waves sea-
levelled shor

ed-awaken
ings.

Early spring

rain may wash
once delicate

ly refined
memories a

way but
their image

(however less
ened) may re

turn at the
most necess

ary recalling-
time

s.

Time-offer

ings Even as
the body

hurts and e
ven decay

s these
words will re

fashion their
once substan

cial time-
offering

s.

The Half-way

type He'd
never been

the half-
way type

though age
revealed its

more cautious
ways His card

s remained
(even from

the first-
day-on) fully-

exposed-on-
the-table Per

haps that
would lead to

more-open-
wounds he

felt well-be
fore his a

ging-year
s.

Lowering-down

You knew
where you

stood–with–
him even

from–the–
first but

better not
too–highly–

sourced or
that special

ing look–of–
his would

soon be lower
ing–you–down.

The Route

unexplored
until then

hardly known
as with Colum

bus' not even
correctly-

mapped–out
but in time

it became e
ased in to

a much desir
ed semi–trop

cal–find.

History den

ies (as Ranke
showed us)

what never oc
curred but e

ven–more–so
the mind's

still–activat
ed–imagining

s.

Time-length

ed As a child
I used to lis

ten for the
very early

mysterious
sounds of

the distant
trains between

station
s then bey

ond my child
hood time–

length.

Explanation

not justifi
cation As

Kiev remains
the first and

holy capital
of the pan–

Slavic
cause while

Ukrainian
s who don't

accept that
treated as

traitors ex
plains Putin'

s sub–human
behavior but

doesn't justi
fy–it.

Is the Ameri

can continu

ous support
of Western

European de
mocracies

since The
Great War

not only ideo
logical but ego

istic as well
For many Ameri

cans our nat
ion's an his

torical contin
uation of its

founding fa
thers despite

Washington's
Farewell Add

ress But then
even the Brit

ish find–it–
difficult to

accept Ameri
can deviation

s The post–
Washington–

long–political–
isolation

never complete
ly cancelled

our cultural
and even polit

ical dependen
cy despite

Manifest Des
tiny.

Self-destruc

tive imperial
powers whether

Roman British
French Ger

man and Russian
man come and

go blood-sancti
fying their na

tion's ideologi
cal-superior

ity.

National

ism and nation
al–causes

have remain
ed historical

ly the great
est enemy of

genuine Christ
ianity despite

an–apparent–
partner

ship–basis.

Individual

ism's higher
claims have

generally
been levelled–

down to a
self–achiev

ing–loneli
ness.

The Feminist

If she's
robbed him

of all-
means-of-de

fense person
al and histor

ical There's
only one final

resort "Don't
hit-a-man

when-he's-
down."

April 1st

day with all

the first
flowers and

tree-blossom
ing display

ing the full-
range-of-their-

radiant-
coloring

s neverthe
less a sad

April 1st
day.

The Godly

Israel model
of chosen

ness continu
ally renamed

by other na
tions for

themselves
mostly implicit

ly universal
istic.

Tip-a Canoe

and Tyler-too
"Ike looks

good on a
mik" as the

original
brand Dickens'

Pickwick Papers
for the Elect

ion of 1832
displaying

the lowest
(bought) le

vels of Anglo-
American demo

cracy.

Another

sunless-
drab day

The early
spring flow

ers dulled
of their pre

suming-intent
Even these

words seem
less occasion

ed for their
time-inherent

precision.

Another

Pall-bearing
Friday as if

I could be
lifted to the

height of
residual hand-

lengthened-
aspiring

s.

Futureless

when fewer
young ladie

s willing
to burden

themselves
s with child

ren birthed
to those pro

blematic
ages when

family's lost
its self-se

curing–protect
iveness–claim

s What's be
come of a

work and play
society's

individual
ist comfort

s.

Russia

How does one
realise the

highest liter
ary culture

of modern
times and a

socialistic
(now fascist

ic society)
denying the

otherwise
individual

ism of a Tol
stoy Dostoyev

sky Turgen
ev and Chekh

ov.

Alone in an

empty house
unable to

hear correct
ly The door

unlocked
sounds like

an open in
vitation for

a steathy walk
er-in.

Families

first remains
in many so-

called "primit
ive" societie

s (not only Mus
lim) the larger

protective
family broken-

down in the
name of indiv

idualism and
progress Now

the tradition
al family

loosening
its time-

hold replaced
by mongrel fam

ilies of a dis
cordant-reach

or no-family-
at-all alone

familiness
Godless man

in his origin
ally pre-form

ing lonely naked-
state.

Individual

ism and ego
ism two appar

ently inter
changeable

causes Do
what you like

and please
call it in

the name of
some-higher-

cause.

The German

pre-Fontane
19th century

novel with the
various theor

ies of the
novel's pre-

determining-
course Roman

tic Bieder
meier Real

ist ... Even
poetically

cross-roaded
as with Adal

bert Stifter
while rarely

personally
flesh and blood

ed in a gen
uine social-

context The
path for a

later realised
de-humanised-

society?

We're all

gifted with
our special

(if also
time-chosen)

right-of-
way usually

created at
the cost of

"those road
s not taken"

Many critics
propagate

that as their
"special

truth".

Tchaikovsky'

s 1st Quartet
an early work

uneases me
for my taste

his only gen
uine-chamber-

music-work
so well idiomat

ically-conceiv
ed at the al

most total loss
of essential-

individual
ity.

Why should

Ravel capable
as few impress

ionists (at
least for my

taste) of creat
ing truly great

existential
ly-expressive-

music be most
ly satisfied

with orches
tral brill

iant-indiv
iduality.

Mozart

if necessary
could match–

up to the
very best of

Haydn's string
quartets

whereas the
generation–

elder-Haydn
could compose

mature concerti
of Mozart's

poetic-best
Yet despite

their encom
passing gen

ius each re
mained large

ly within his
own appropri

ated–sphere
s.

Some major

artists grow
through their

own intuitive
ly subject

ive develop
ment Others

more from out
side influence

s Even the
greatest of

innovators
Haydn rejected

late-in-life
his fine and

highly individ
ualistic Opus

1 string quar
tets as a more

or less "stud
ent work"

For a "classi
cal poet" of

essential word-
reductive trans

parency The
highly theatri

cal display of
most operas

leaves him at-
best mostly-

disinterest
ed.

Neo-Classi

cal remains
for me whe

ther of the
Stravinsky-

type or the
Carracci Broth

ers artificial
ly-imitat

ive.

Much of late

romantic music'
s not only

bombastic re
maining in its

big-mouthed-
orientat

ion distant
from the soul

ed-intimacy
of chamber mus

ic-like express
iveness.

Is it the

> same Brahms of
> impersonal
>
> piano-solo mus
> ic and his
>
> deeply-souled-
> spiritual
>
> works espec
> ially his
>
> Requiem.

There's some

> thing truly
> Mozartean in
>
> Chopin's best
> most-intimate
>
> ly-personal-
> works yet
>
> his finger-
> proclaiming
>
> sound-calls
> and romantic
>
> moon-lit sat
> urated works
>
> mostly put-
> me-off.

Cherubini

(though not
of Haydn's his

role-model's
stature) re

mains a compos
er most necess

ary to be re-
discovered

after Schumann'
s self-center

ed romantic in
terpretat

ions – most es
pecially his

early masses
and the inter

esting very
late string

quartets and
quintets.

In Nomine
Domini
March 3, 2023

Poetry books by David Jaffin

1. **Conformed to Stone,** Abelard-Schuman, New York 1968, London 1970.

2. **Emptied Spaces,** with an illustration by Jacques Lipschitz, Abelard-Schuman, London 1972.

3. **In the Glass of Winter,** Abelard-Schuman, London 1975, with an illustration by Mordechai Ardon.

4. **As One,** The Elizabeth Press, New Rochelle, N. Y. 1975.

5. **The Half of a Circle,** The Elizabeth Press, New Rochelle, N. Y. 1977.

6. **Space of,** The Elizabeth Press, New Rochelle, N. Y. 1978.

7. **Preceptions,** The Elizabeth Press, New Rochelle, N. Y. 1979.

8. **For the Finger's Want of Sound,** Shearsman Plymouth, England 1982.

9. **The Density for Color,** Shearsman Plymouth, England 1982.

10. **Selected Poems** with an illustration by Mordechai Ardon, English/Hebrew, Massada Publishers, Givatyim, Israel 1982.

11. **The Telling of Time,** Shearsman Books, Kentisbeare, England 2000 and Johannis, Lahr, Germany.

12. **That Sense for Meaning,** Shearsman Books, Kentisbeare, England 2001 and Johannis, Lahr, Germany.

13. **Into the timeless Deep,** Shearsman Books, Kentisbeare, England 2003 and Johannis, Lahr, Germany.

14. **A Birth in Seeing,** Shearsman Books, Exeter, England 2003 and Johannis, Lahr, Germany.

15. **Through Lost Silences,** Shearsman Books, Exeter, England 2003 and Johannis, Lahr, Germany.

16. **A voiced Awakening,** Shearsman Books, Exter, England 2004 and Johannis, Lahr, Germany.

17. **These Time-Shifting Thoughts**, Shearsman Books, Exeter, England 2005 and Johannis, Lahr, Germany.

18. **Intimacies of Sound,** Shearsman Books, Exeter, England 2005 and Johannis, Lahr, Germany.

19. **Dream Flow** with an illustration by Charles Seliger, Shearsman Books, Exeter, England 2006 and Johannis, Lahr, Germany.

20. **Sunstreams** with an illustration by Charles Seliger, Shearsman Books, Exeter, England 2007 and Johannis, Lahr, Germany.

21. **Thought Colors,** with an illustration by Charles Seliger, Shearsman Books, Exeter, England 2008 and Johannis, Lahr, Germany.

22. **Eye-Sensing,** Ahadada, Tokyo, Japan and Toronto, Canada 2008.

23. **Wind-phrasings,** with an illustration by Charles Seliger, Shearsman Books, Exeter, England 2009 and Johannis, Lahr, Germany.

24. **Time shadows,** with an illustration by Charles Seliger, Shearsman Books, Exeter, England 2009 and Johannis, Lahr, Germany.

25. **A World mapped-out,** with an illustration by Charles Seliger, Shearsman Books, Exeter, England 2010.

26. **Light Paths,** with an illustration by Charles Seliger, Shearsman Books, Exeter, England 2011 and Edition Wortschatz, Schwarzenfeld, Germany.

27. **Always Now,** with an illustration by Charles Seliger, Shearsman Books, Bristol, England 2012 and Edition Wortschatz, Schwarzenfeld, Germany.

28. **Labyrinthed,** with an illustration by Charles Seliger, Shearsman Books, Bristol, England 2012 and Edition Wortschatz, Schwarzenfeld, Germany.

29. **The Other Side of Self,** with an illustration by Charles Seliger, Shearsman Books, Bristol, England 2012 and Edition Wortschatz, Schwarzenfeld, Germany.

30. **Light Sources,** with an illustration by Charles Seliger, Shearsman Books, Bristol, England 2013 and Edition Wortschatz, Schwarzenfeld, Germany.

31. **Landing Rights,** with an illustration by Charles Seliger, Shearsman Books, Bristol, England 2014 and Edition Wortschatz, Schwarzenfeld, Germany.

32. **Listening to Silence,** with an illustration by Charles Seliger, Shearsman Books, Bristol, England 2014 and Edition Wortschatz, Schwarzenfeld, Germany.

33. **Taking Leave,** with an illustration by Mei Fêng, Shearsman Books, Bristol, England 2014 and Edition Wortschatz, Schwarzenfeld, Germany.

34. **Jewel Sensed,** with an illustration by Paul Klee, Shearsman Books, Bristol, England 2015 and Edition Wortschatz, Schwarzenfeld, Germany.

35. **Shadowing Images**, with an illustration by Pieter de Hooch, Shearsman Books, Bristol, England 2015 and Edition Wortschatz, Schwarzenfeld.

36. **Untouched Silences**, with an illustration by Paul Seehaus, Shearsman Books, Bristol, England 2016 and Edition Wortschatz, Schwarzenfeld.

37. **Soundlesss Impressions**, with an illustration by Qi Baishi, Shearsman Books, Bristol, England 2016 and Edition Wortschatz, Schwarzenfeld.

38. **Moon Flowers**, with a photograph by Hannelore Bäumler, Shearsman Books, Bristol, England 2017 and Edition Wortschatz, Schwarzenfeld.

39. **The Healing of a Broken World**, with a photograph by Hannelore Bäumler, Shearsman Books, Bristol, England 2018 and Edition Wortschatz, Cuxhaven.

40. **Opus 40**, with a photograph by Hannelore Bäumler, Shearsman Books, Bristol, England 2018 and Edition Wortschatz, Cuxhaven.

41. **Identity Cause**, with a photograph by Hannelore Bäumler, Shearsman Books, Bristol, England 2018 and Edition Wortschatz, Cuxhaven.

42. **Kaleidoscope**, with a photograph by Hannelore Bäumler, Shearsman Books, Bristol, England 2019 and Edition Wortschatz, Cuxhaven.

43. **Snow-touched Imaginings**, with a photograph by Hannelore Bäumler, Shearsman Books, Bristol, England 2019 and Edition Wortschatz, Cuxhaven.

44. **Two-timed**, with a photograph by Hannelore Bäumler, Shearsman Books, Bristol, England 2020 and Edition Wortschatz, Cuxhaven.

45. **Corona Poems**, with a photograph by Hannelore Bäumler, Shearsman Books, Bristol, England 2020 and Edition Wortschatz, Cuxhaven.

46. **Spring Shadowings**, with a photograph by Hannelore Bäumler, Shearsman Books, Bristol, England 2021 and Edition Wortschatz, Cuxhaven.

47. **October: Cyprus Poems**, with an illustration by Odilon Redon, Shearsman Books, Bristol, England 2021 and Edition Wortschatz, Cuxhaven.

48. **Snow Dreams**, with a photograph by Hannelore Bäumler, Shearsman Books, Bristol, England 2022 and Edition Wortschatz, Cuxhaven.

49. **Ukraine Poems**, with a painting by Alfons Röllinger, Shearsman Books, Bristol, England 2022 and Edition Wortschatz, Cuxhaven.

50. **Simply Living Life**,with a photograph by Hannelore Bäumler, Shearsman Books, Bristol, England 2023 and Edition Wortschatz, Cuxhaven.

Book on David Jaffin's poetry: Warren Fulton, **Poemed on a beach,** Ahadada, Tokyo, Japan and Toronto, Canada 2010.